THE CROSSROADS
OF ARKANSAS

THE CROSSROADS OF ARKANSAS

A ONE-HOUR ARKANSAS PERSPECTIVE

John P. Gill

T•H•E
BUTLER
CENTER
FOR ARKANSAS STUDIES
BOOK SERIES

LITTLE ROCK

Published 2001
By The Butler Center for Arkansas Studies
   The Central Arkansas Library System
   100 Rock Street
   Little Rock, Arkansas 72201

Printed in the United States of America
10 9 8 7 6 5 4 3 2 1

Library of Congress Cataloging-in-Publication Data

Gill, John Purifoy.
   The crossroads of Arkansas : a one hour Arkansas perspective / John P. Gill.
      p. cm.
   Originally published: Little Rock : Butler Center Series, 2001.
   Includes bibliographical references.
   ISBN 0-9708574-0-3 (pbk. : alk. paper)
   1. Arkansas—History. I. Title.

F411 .G55 2001
976.7—dc21

Project Editor: Jody McNeese Keene
Designer: H. K. Stewart
Cover Photographs: John P. Gill
Front Cover: The Arkansas state capitol
Back Cover: The dome of the capitol, as seen from the foyer

The paper used in this publication
meets the minimum requirements of the
American National Standard for Information Sciences—
Permanence of Paper for Printed Library Materials,
ANSI Z39.48-1984.

CONTENTS

ARKANSAS COUNTIES

FOREWORD

No state in the nation is so little studied as Arkansas. Our ancestors did not take time to create historical societies and research collections. Only rarely were family records kept through the generations. We did not get a university press until 1980. We did not even include Arkansas history in the state school curriculum until 1997.

Some might believe that because we have neglected our history that we must not have much of a heritage in the first place. Such is not the case! Arkansas is a fascinating place. In many ways our state is a microcosm of American history. We were a colony at one time; a Revolutionary War battle was fought here; slavery left a tragic scar; our western border was a frontier for generations; and the agony of the Great Depression was felt by every Arkansan. The 1957 Crisis was front page news around the world; and in more recent years whole Arkansas families have emerged as world class business leaders. We even produced a president of the United States!

This unfortunate habit of neglecting our rich heritage was a motivating factor in the creation of the Butler Center in 1997. The late Richard C. Butler, Sr., the benefactor of the Butler Center, was proud of his home state and home town, and he wanted Arkansans to take time to learn about and celebrate their heritage. The Butler Center works hard to make this possible.

With the publication of this volume, the Center inaugurates its book series. It is only appropriate that we begin our publications program with a brief survey of the state by John P. Gill, an attorney and resident of Little Rock. This short survey will give our people—as well as visitors—an opportunity to ground themselves in the general historical outline of the state. From this introduction readers can move on to reading more fully about other aspects of our history.

Our book series is designed to produce concise works of Arkansas nonfiction. We will work to publish good quality books that are affordably priced. We invite everyone to read this book. If you like it, please give copies to others.

—Tom W. Dillard
Curator,
The Butler Center
for Arkansas Studies

PREFACE

This book is a one-hour read about Arkansas, its history, and its presence, as seen from the present site of the state capitol—a knoll overlooking the Arkansas River near its intersection with the ancient Southwest Trail. The purpose of this text is to familiarize newcomers with their adoptive state and to give students (young and old) a brief overview of who Arkansawyers are, thereby encouraging further study of this mystical and wonderful place called Arkansas. For more detailed reading, references in the end notes are suggested.

Material for this book is based upon the author's familiarity with Arkansas history and his Arkansiana collection and library, supplemented by research from the archives of the Butler Center for Arkansas Studies of the Central Arkansas Library. The author is grateful for the advice and counsel of Tom W. Dillard, the curator of the Butler Center.

Selected Arkansas cities

Mountain Home

Fayetteville

Jonesboro

Fort Smith

Little Rock

Hot Springs

Helena

Pine Bluff

Camden

Monticello

Texarkana

El Dorado

INTRODUCTION

History is very much like a lawsuit: both attempt to find truth from past events. A trial—be it for divorce, car wreck, or murder—must of necessity deal with past (i.e., historical) events as seen through the eyes of different witnesses. Some will say the light was red. Some will say it was green. Others will say it changed.

So it is with history—the witnesses view places, people, and events differently. Writers of history therefore have a difficult task and, like jurors at a trial, should give all views of historical events equal weight, before pronouncing the final judgment—the truth as the historian sees it. To attempt to condense a history covering several centuries of a place and people as varied as Arkansas is therefore a high risk venture.

For example, is Arkansawyer Bear Bryant the winningest coach in college football, as is often stated? Actually, Eddie Robinson at Grambling won more games, but Bryant was the winningest coach in Division I, or the big leagues where the national championships are found. And Bryant—three-time coach of the year—won fifteen conference titles, made twenty-nine bowl appearances, and won six national championships. To be precise, the phrase should be written the "winningest coach in

Division I college football," but that takes more space and this is a condensed history. So, certain editorial privilege is exercised in this attempt to give the reader a quick read on one of the most interesting places on earth—Arkansas.

For the sake of space, these comments are cryptic in terms of a full explanation of history, and readers may disagree with some points. But at least the reader may be enticed to learn more about the Parkin Mounds, Patrick Cleburne, Scipio Jones, and this exciting place called Arkansas.

THE CROSSROADS OF ARKANSAS

Built in 1911 near the exact center of the state, Arkansas' state capitol sits at the crossroads of Arkansas. From the front lawn, the land to the east and south is flat prairie and delta, dropping only two hundred feet all the way to the Gulf of Mexico. From the rear windows, the Arkansas River opens the gateway to the West between the Ouachita Mountains to the southwest and the Ozark Mountains to the north. A few blocks away sits the "little rock," the first rock outcropping upriver from the Mississippi and the namesake for Arkansas' capitol city.

Arkansas has many paradoxes. It is the smallest state west of the Mississippi, yet it has more miles of river navigable by steamboat than any other state in the nation. On the date of the Declaration of Independence, Arkansas was a Spanish colony, far removed from Philadelphia, yet one of two battles in the American Revolution fought west of the Mississippi (and thus on foreign soil) was in southeast Arkansas at Arkansas Post. Arkansas was never an English colony, yet, while Louisiana adopted (and still uses) the civil law of continental Europe, English common law was adopted for the original Arkansas counties, thereby setting the precedent for using English common law in the other states created from the Louisiana Purchase and the rest of the western United States.

The Arkansas home of the late Sam Walton, America's richest man in the late twentieth century, is a different Arkansas from the sixteenth-century wilderness of Hernando de Soto. Colonized, poor, and isolated for much of its history, few places are as misrepresented and misunderstood as Arkansas.

PRE-COLUMBIAN ARKANSAS

Geography kept Arkansas isolated for decades. Its vast river system flows to the southeast and enters the Mississippi near the state's southern border. Westward migration down the Ohio, Cumberland, and other eastern rivers required travelers to descend the Mississippi great distances if they were to use the Arkansas, White, and St. Francis rivers and nearly to Baton Rouge to use the Ouachita and Red rivers. Instead, most settlers followed the Missouri, Platte, and other northern tributaries of the Mississippi, some of which provided transportation almost due west. Additionally, the vast lowlands along the Mississippi delta stretched in places over one hundred miles to the Ouachitas and Ozarks. Delta floods, mosquitoes, canebrakes, and thick vegetation made westward movement across Arkansas next to impossible during the long months of wet weather.

One geographic anomaly is the unique Crowley's Ridge. Unlike most mountains, which nature created by violent upheavals, volcanoes, or earthquakes, Crowley's Ridge is the result of wind-blown dust that accumulated over the ages. The deep ravines that crisscross the ridge proved to be an equally difficult barrier for westward movement. Not until the railroads developed after the Civil War did settlers stream into Arkansas.

Long before the railroads came to the Arkansas wilderness, these forbidding eastern lowlands were the home of migrating hunters. The Sloan site in the Cache River flood plain near Paragould, dating from 8500 B.C., is the oldest documented burial

MAJOR ARKANSAS RIVERS

ground in the New World.[1] By 900 A.D., during the Temple Mound Period, the Arkansas Indians of the Mississippian cultures were one of the great Pre-Columbian civilizations of North America. They developed intensive agriculture and settled in villages in which beautiful pottery, sculpture, and intricate beadwork were crafted. They built mounds for temples of worship and government. Two large sites still exist: one not too far east of the capitol, at Toltec near the Arkansas River, and another at Parkin on the St. Francis River. Both mounds were fortified, Parkin with a moat and Toltec with an earthen wall.[2]

Among the first Arkansas Indians to encounter Europeans were the Quapaw, who numbered more than twenty thousand people at the time and constituted a formidable force of military strength. Various historic accounts describe the Quapaw as tall, handsome, well-mannered, liberal, peace-loving, good humored, excellent fighters, brave, skilled boatmen, magnificent craftsmen, great hunters, and good swimmers. Early maps described their area as "the land of the handsome men."[3] Their dugout canoes were sought after by Europeans. The French and the Spanish actively sought political and economic alliance with the Quapaw.[4]

THE FIRST EXPLORERS

Spaniard Hernando de Soto and his conquistadors became the first Europeans to enter Arkansas, crossing the Mississippi in 1541—fifty years after Columbus discovered America. de Soto died during his exploration of Arkansas and was buried secretly in southern Arkansas.[5] Over 125 years later, the French became the next Europeans to explore the area. First Marquette and Joliet explored the Mississippi as far south as the mouth of the Arkansas. In 1682 came La Salle, who claimed the entire Mississippi Valley for France, and later Henri de Tonti, an Italian agent of the French known as the father of Arkansas, established the first white settlement at Arkansas Post in 1686 amid the villages of the Quapaw near the confluence of the Arkansas and Mississippi rivers.[6] In 1722, as part of the French effort to expand trade, La Harpe explored the Arkansas River and found the "big rock" across the river from the "little rock."

The Quapaw became valued and loyal allies of the French explorers. The French were impressed by the friendliness of the Quapaw tribe, whom they called the *Akansa* or *Arkansas*, thus giving the state its name.[7]

Hernando de Soto in the Ouachita Mountains, from the painting by Maurice Kellogg, published with permission of Julia Hughes Jones, former State Auditor.

For a time, the French held high hopes for the area. The French Indian Company built cities in Mobile, Natchez, and New Orleans, but their most ambitious plans were reserved for the Arkansas River Valley, in what was to be the personal fiefdom of John Law, the company's director. Unfortunately, Law went bankrupt, and his "Mississippi bubble" burst.[8]

When France lost the Seven Years' War in 1763, it ceded its Arkansas colony and all other possessions west of the Mississippi to Spain, and all its possessions east to England. As the Quapaw had protected the French colony from the Chickasaw and their English allies, the Quapaw protected Spain from the Osage. Spain held Arkansas during America's war for independence, and while the United States Constitution was drafted, Arkansas was ruled by a Spanish governor in New Orleans.

THE LOUISIANA PURCHASE

With the dawn of the nineteenth century, Spain ceded the vast Louisiana Territory back to France, and for two years, Napoleon was the emperor of Arkansas. When Thomas Jefferson completed the Louisiana Purchase from France in 1803, the first Arkansawyers—the Quapaw—had successfully kept the area intact so that it was never parceled out among France, England, or Spain. In 1815, President James Madison commissioned Prospect Robbins and Joseph Brown to survey the Louisiana Purchase, and their benchmark at the intersection of present-day Monroe, Lee, and Phillips counties is the point from which every farm and home from Arkansas to Montana is measured.

Between France and Spain, the two countries had maintained a presence at Arkansas Post for more than a century. However, frequent flooding, mosquitoes, Indian attacks, and epidemics prevented the colony from flourishing.[9] Throughout this time and for over a decade following the Louisiana Purchase, Arkansas remained almost exclusively the province of rugged hunters and fur traders who spread out upon the area's many rivers in their quest for furs, skins, tallow, and bear oil.[10]

This isolation proved advantageous in at least one respect. In December 1811, the New Madrid earthquake, the greatest earthquake in historical times in North America, sent shocks throughout the mid-Mississippi Valley. The earthquake created huge depressions—the sunken lands in the St. Francis River Basin in northeast Arkansas—yet little injury occurred in the remote Arkansas wilderness. People displaced by the earthquake were given New Madrid certificates for title to new lands, and several settled within sight of where the capitol would later stand.

To examine America's new purchase, Dunbar, Hunter, Schoolcraft, Featherstonhaugh, Gerstaecker, and the noted botanist Thomas Nutall explored Arkansas. Settlers followed, and with them came adventurers and land speculators who created new town sites. One of the new arrivals, William E. Woodruff, began printing the *Arkansas Gazette* in 1819.[11] The newspaper (although since then acquired by another) is still published just a few blocks from the capitol, and its heritage is the oldest newspaper west of the Mississippi. The new territory also drew another aspiring breed—young politicians ambitious to carve a power base for themselves. More often than not, personal insults took precedence over political ideology. Quite frequently, to be successful, candidates had to triumph not only at the polls, but also survive the subsequent duel.[12]

SETTLING THE WILDERNESS

The mid-1830s saw the publication of the nation's first dime novel masquerading as nonfiction. This inflammatory account of the exploits and plans of Arkansas outlaw John Murrell and his alleged army of criminal minions spawned an outbreak of vigilante violence throughout the lower Mississippi Valley.[13] Even the *Arkansas Gazette* called for lynching "by prudent and respectable persons," urging that criminals "be hunted down as wild beasts, and their carcasses left as food for the buzzards."[14] So-called "regulators" scoured Arkansas of its less desirable elements. Many, of course, migrated to Texas.

Another group affected by the encroachment of settlers was Arkansas' Indians. The ink on the Louisiana Purchase had scarcely dried before Thomas Jefferson and subsequent presidents began to look upon Arkansas as a potential dumping ground for eastern tribes crowded out by white settlements in the eastern United States. The Cherokee were the first to accept in large numbers the offer of new homes in Arkansas.[15] After centuries of commerce with whites, they differed little in their tools, weapons, dwellings, and material culture from the Arkansas hunters who were their contemporaries. In 1817, the federal government recognized the Cherokee's Arkansas holdings in a formal treaty. This prompted a new wave of Indian immigration, including many wealthy, missionary-influenced, and educated planters and stock raisers. One such Cherokee was Chief Jolly, who arrived in 1818 at the command of 17 keelboats crowded with 331 followers and slaves.[16] While he remained in Arkansas during the 1820s, Jolly in all likelihood was the wealthiest man in the territory.

Chief John Jolly (Ooloo-Tee-Skee), after a sketch by George Catlin.

One of the most unexpected facets of Arkansas' history is that so many of the "pioneers" who helped civilize the Arkansas wilderness were in fact Indians. The Cherokee cleared much of the land north of the Arkansas River, and many present-day towns have sprung up on the sites of their former villages. The Cherokee founded the first school in Arkansas, and the first steamboat to navigate the Arkansas as far as Little Rock carried supplies for the Cherokee mission.[17] The first sermon preached in Little Rock was delivered by a missionary to the Cherokee.[18] Near Russellville, a Cherokee named Sequoyah invented the Cherokee alphabet to permit his people and the whites to communicate, becoming the first person in history to single-handedly invent an alphabet.[19]

Arkansas was initially part of the Louisiana Territory, then part of the Missouri Territory, and in 1819, the federal government created the Arkansas Territory. The vagaries of U.S. Indian policy came to a boiling point the following year, when the federal government decided to relocate the Choctaw Indians to the area between the Arkansas and Red rivers, then the fastest-growing region of Arkansas. The governor estimated that nearly a third of the entire white population of Arkansas faced eviction.[20] The resistance of the settlers at times bordered on armed insurrection, and the Choctaws were eventually moved farther west.

The Choctaw fiasco united Arkansas against U.S. Indian policy, and the Quapaw were the first to suffer the consequences. Although the tribe was well respected and prided itself on never having shed the blood of whites, the Quapaw were forced to sell their land and leave Arkansas. The territorial legislature then turned its attention to the Cherokee, declaring the tribe's hunting preserve a county and opening it to white settlement.[21] Eager for a solution that would placate both Indians and whites, President John Quincy Adams offered to exchange the Cherokee preserve for lands in present-day Oklahoma, then part of the Arkansas Territory. Tempers soon cooled and the tribe relocated peacefully. The Arkansas Cherokee never experienced the more brutal coercion of their eastern kin associated with the infamous Trail of Tears, one route of which in the 1830s passed by the site where Arkansas' first state capitol would later be constructed.[22] By 1830, all Indian tribes had been removed from Arkansas, and the Choctaw and Cherokee lines had established the new western border.[23]

THE TWO CULTURES OF ARKANSAS

Even though the Arkansas Territory included most of present-day Oklahoma as well as Arkansas, the original capitol was at Arkansas Post. It was soon moved to Little Rock, but no one knows where the territorial government's offices were situated. There is a popular belief that the legislature met in the Hinderliter Tavern at the present Arkansas Territorial Restoration, but the only documented fact is that some meetings were held at the Baptist Meeting House. When Arkansas became a state in 1836, state government moved into a new capitol building on the bank of the Arkansas River at Little Rock. Now known as the Old State House, it is arguably the most historic building in Arkansas and one of the nation's finest examples of Greek Revival architecture.

Well before its statehood, Arkansas was known outside its borders. For example, a French map printed in 1832 showed only twenty-four cities in what is now the United States; one of them was "Arkopolis," the former name for Little Rock. Within its borders, however, this new state wasn't one place at all, but two. Nature and geography had conspired to create two separate and distinct environments which had given rise to two radically distinct cultures: the mountains and the delta.

The mountain highlands grew rapidly in the decades prior to the Civil War, but life was rugged in these "hardscrabble hills," where farming rocky soil was a challenge. Corn was the universal crop, although a considerable amount of wheat was grown in the northwest. Many raised cattle, horses, and mules, and almost everyone raised hogs. It was said the typical Ozark hog was mean enough to scare a wolf and so skinny you could shave with its backbone: the "razorback."

Highlanders were a fairly homogeneous group. Generally of English and Scotch-Irish heritage, with a smattering of German, most hailed from the uplands of Tennessee, Kentucky, Missouri, and the Carolinas. Many had been born and bred on the American frontier. Though their settlements were widely scattered, the harsh necessities of frontier life bound them together. If a family had land to clear or needed to build a shelter, they held a house raising, and people came from miles around to lend a hand. Such affairs usually culminated in a hoedown, with music supplied by the ubiquitous fiddle. Shooting matches, quilting parties, and religious camp meetings also brought people together. The few stores that existed formed the nucleus of the fledgling mountain towns. These shops, known as "doggeries" because of the many hounds lying outside, often served as saloon, inn, post office, church, polling place, and courthouse as well.[24]

The highlands were decidedly western in outlook. Nowhere was this more evident than the twin trading centers of Fort Smith and Van Buren, the only link to the outside world for much of the region. Fort Smith's significance to the American west is best demonstrated by the fact that the U.S. Army's most elite infantry unit was stationed there.[25] Perched on the edge of the frontier, these twin cities emerged in 1849 as an important jumping-off point for the California gold rush.[26] The region began to dream of being chosen as the route for the proposed transcontinental railroad. Small wonder highlanders turned a deaf ear to the increasingly strident secessionist sentiments beginning to be voiced in the delta.

Arkansas' lowlands were developing at the same time. With armies of slaves performing the backbreaking labor necessary to clear the countless trees and unending canebrakes, portions of the delta yielded to cotton plantations. Too often we overlook the role played by black Arkansawyers in the taming of the Arkansas wilderness. Slavery was an inherently brutal system, but we lose sight of the contribution of slaves in the development of the delta if we reduce them to the one-dimensional status of victims. Slaves not only served as laborers and field hands, but they also performed skilled tasks necessary to keep the plantations functioning. Among the skilled craftsmen were carpenters, mechanics, wagon makers, seamstresses, cooks, and blacksmiths. Slaves took part in management, and almost every large plantation had black foremen and crew bosses. A few had black overseers.[27]

Rivers were the veins and arteries of the delta. Even before the dawn of steamboats, traders plied Arkansas' rivers in keelboats. By offering seed and supplies on consignment, delta entrepreneurs helped found the fledgling cotton industry, and the keelboats soon gave way to hundreds of steamboats hauling cotton to market and importing manufactured goods.

The rich lowland soil attracted Italians, Scandinavians, Germans, and other Europeans, as well as many younger sons of old planter families east of the Mississippi. They came to colonize Arkansas for the plantation system. As planters grew in wealth and influence, many built their splendid town houses in the cultural meccas of the many lively cotton ports that sprang up in towns such as Camden, Helena, Lake Village, Pine Bluff, and Jacksonport. Here Arkansas developed its form of the cultural grandeur of the Old South. And it was here that the ideas of the Deep South would find a receptive audience.

THE CIVIL WAR

Proclaiming "God in his omnipotent wisdom, I believe, created the cotton plant, the African slave and the Mississippi Valley to clothe and feed the world, and the gallant race of men and women upon its soil to defend it and execute that decree,"[28] Henry Massie Rector was elected governor the same year voters propelled Abraham Lincoln to the presidency. Arkansas faced the national crisis that followed with perhaps the lamest elected leadership in its history.

Almost immediately, the secessionists sought to take Arkansas out of the Union. Although they lacked sufficient strength in the legislature, they managed to call a special convention to consider the issue. The election of delegates was as close as Arkansas would ever come to polling the population on this controversial issue. The secessionists were well financed, well organized, and held a monopoly of statewide elected officials. Nevertheless, when the convention was called to order, it soon became apparent that pro-unionists held an unshakeable majority, and the forces of the highlands and their allies from key geographic swing areas—such as Little Rock—rejected secession.[29]

Forces were at work, however, that were beyond Arkansas' control. The Civil War began as fighting erupted at Fort Sumter in South Carolina, and Lincoln issued a call for Arkansas troops to help put down the rebellion.[30] All hope of neutrality was dashed. The price of remaining in the Union was to bear arms against friends and kinsmen in states from which so many Arkansawyers had emigrated. The convention reconvened, and this time a nearly unanimous majority favored secession. A woman in the balcony showered the lone dissenter, Isaac Murphy, with flowers.

Arkansas was at war. In the cottonports, Confederate units were mustered with great fanfare to the tunes of brass bands, while the women composed poems, stitched battle flags, and garlanded the troops with flowers. At the same time, Union sympathizers from the Ozarks were marched to Little Rock in chains. Despite its reluctance to enter the fray, Arkansas supplied more troops per capita to the Southern cause than any state besides South Carolina and Virginia. By the same token, more Arkansas citizens bore arms for the Union than those of any other Confederate state besides Tennessee.[31] The war tore Arkansas apart and inflicted wounds that took generations to heal.

Most of the Confederate troops from Arkansas were shipped off to the battlefields east of the Mississippi, leaving the state almost defenseless. The severity of this drain of native sons is perhaps best illustrated by the fact that the Confederacy's best division commander, Major General Patrick R. Cleburne of Helena, fought at Chattanooga, Atlanta, and Franklin, Tennessee—not in Arkansas.[32]

Confederate forces in Arkansas displayed daring and brilliant tactics, but at best the campaigns were counted a draw, and the South needed a win. For example, while the biggest battle west of the Mississippi River—at Pea Ridge—was a draw, it left Missouri in the Union and opened north Arkansas to Union forces.

Little Rock fell in 1863 when the Union flanked Confederate troops and crossed the Arkansas River, under sporadic fire, on a pontoon bridge. Because of the maneuver, Little Rock was spared the destruction suffered by so many other Southern cities.[33] After Little Rock fell, Arkansas' Confederate state capitol was relocated to the Hempstead County courthouse at Washington, Arkansas. The town had already carved its name in history in the 1830s when James Black crafted the original Bowie knife there, and Sam Houston and others met there to plan the Texas Revolution.[34]

The Confederacy's only real Arkansas success came during the Red River Campaign when Union supply trains were captured, causing a Union retreat to Little Rock, which left southwest Arkansas in Confederate hands throughout the War.[35]

Although the land battles were not decisive, two naval incidents were spectacular. It is said the most destructive single shot fired during the Civil War occurred near St. Charles on the White River, when a shell from a Confederate battery struck the boiler on the Union gunboat *Mound City*, causing an explosion that destroyed the ship.[36] The deadliest maritime accident in American history, with the greatest loss of life until the sinking of the *Titanic*, occurred off Fogleman's Landing on the Mississippi River, nine miles north of present-day West Memphis, when more than fifteen hundred recently freed Union POWS died after

Sinking of the Sultana near Fogleman's Landing, from a sketch by Richard De Spain, published with permission of Arkansas Chief Justice John A. Fogleman, retired.

the river boat *Sultana* exploded and sank October 27, 1865, only months after the war's end.[37]

Although removed to the Indian Territory west of Arkansas, native Americans continued to influence Arkansas history. On June 23, 1865, two months after Lee surrendered at Appomattox, the only Indian general on either side, Stan Watie, who had led the attack that captured the Union artillery at Pea Ridge, became the last Confederate general to surrender.[38]

RECONSTRUCTION

The Arkansas economy was destroyed by the war. In antebellum Arkansas, the average Arkansawyer's income was higher than those in half of all states in the Union—including northern states.[39] After the war, however, a large portion of the male population was dead or disabled, and the civilian population had suffered horribly from the war. The long shadow of Reconstruction cast more suffering and humiliation for generations afterwards, and things might have been far worse were it not for the enlightened attitude of General Frederick Steele, the Union commander in Arkansas.

Steele overcame the outrage incurred by his hanging the "boy martyr" of the Confederacy, seventeen-year-old David O. Dodd, as a spy during the occupation of Little Rock.[40] Steele had once owned a plantation in Arkansas and was familiar with the area; moreover, he opposed a policy of revenge against those who had fought for the Confederacy. When Steele captured Little Rock, he brought with him none other than Isaac Murphy, the sole dissenting delegate from the secession convention. Murphy formed a government of reconciliation in Arkansas, one which would restore the native rule of Arkansas unionists and ex-confederates alike. It was a remarkable undertaking, one of the few "presidential reconstruction" governments formed in the South, so called because it had the support of Abraham Lincoln prior to his assassination. Murphy appealed to the people of Arkansas:

> We have all done wrong. No one can say that his heart is altogether clean…Then as we wish to be forgiven, let us forgive those who have sinned against us and ours. The land is steeped in blood—innocent blood—and defiled with crime. Let us wash it out with tears of sorrow and repentance, works of love, kindness and charity that peace, good will and confidence may return and dwell among us.[41]

But conciliation had no chance with the new Radical Republican majority in Congress, and one of its first acts was to impose a new scheme of "Reconstruction" upon the South that included the refusal to seat Arkansas' congressional delegation.

Reconstruction in Arkansas led to the calling of a constitutional convention, and the chief architect of the new constitution was Joseph Brooks, an abolitionist and Methodist minister who had come to Arkansas as the chaplain of a black infantry detachment. Adoption of the new constitution and the election of officials occurred simultaneously.

Arkansas' Democratic Party was in total disarray. It ran no candidates and many members boycotted the voting entirely. In an election marred by controversy and irregularities, the new constitution was adopted and the Republican Party swept nearly every office. The man to emerge as the party's leader and new governor was Powell Clayton, an ex-Kansas cavalry officer who had parlayed the support of Union veterans to capture the party's top slot.[42]

Few chapters in Arkansas history are as controversial as Reconstruction and its central figure, Powell Clayton. While the Clayton administration inaugurated black voting and greatly expanded public financing of education begun under the Murphy government, the state's fiscal policies almost bankrupted Arkansas in a few short years. Most of the Republicans were from the more affluent and industrialized North and Midwest. They viewed railroads as synonymous with development and attempted to aggressively finance railroad construction by issuing state and local bonds, which placed a staggering debt upon an already ravaged economy.

Even more controversial, however, was the question of political violence. Powell Clayton branded all acts of political terrorism committed by ex-confederates as the workings of a vast and monolithic Ku Klux Klan in Arkansas. While it is undoubtedly true that some former Confederates engaged in violence and intimidation, partisan political considerations came into play, and martial law was declared in several counties, all of which had Democratic political majorities. It was not long, however, before reports began to pour in from the countryside detailing acts of looting, vandalism, violence, and murder committed by the militia while "enforcing" martial law. Clayton proclaimed ten counties to be in a "state of insurrection."[43]

The controversial conduct of the militia, among other things, split the Republican ranks, with native unionists and moderate Republicans on the one hand and radicals on the other. The split gave ex-confederates someplace to hang their hats, and the new moderate coalition presented a serious challenge to the Clayton forces. At one point, Clayton found himself facing impeachment while maneuvering for election by the legislature to the U.S. Senate. Eventually a deal was struck and Clayton received his Senate seat in exchange for promises of election reform and other compromises.

THE BROOKS-BAXTER WAR

All this left the governor's office wide open, and the opposing forces were evenly matched. For governor, the moderates chose none other than Joseph Brooks, the "carpetbagger" who had at one time defended Clayton's militia policy. Clayton's hand-picked candidate was an Arkansas unionist named Elisha Baxter. During the Civil War, Baxter had faced execution under Confederate martial law decrees and managed to survive by escaping from prison in Little Rock. During the period of Clayton's martial law, Baxter was credited with almost single-handedly sparing Batesville and Independence County from destruction at the hands of the militia. This was peculiar politics: both sides had chosen men who, by all rules of logic, should have been the candidates of their opposition.

Joseph Brooks probably won the election of 1872,[44] but the Radicals had a tight grip on the election machinery and declared

Baxter the winner. It was a move they soon came to rue, for
Baxter began almost immediately to dismantle Radical
Reconstruction. As Baxter moved to purge the militia, reform the
election process, and halt the carte blanche issuance of railroad
bonds, political loyalties switched completely. Moderates and ex-
confederates flocked to Baxter, while the Radicals found

*Pine Bluff volunteers embark for Little Rock to reinforce Governor Baxter's forces,
from* Leslies Illustrated Newspaper.

themselves in the ironic position of supporting Brooks' claim of election fraud.

Thus commenced one of the most bizarre episodes of Reconstruction in the South and a colorful chapter in the history of the Old State House—the Brooks-Baxter War.[45] The State Supreme Court had already affirmed Baxter's election, so Brooks took his case before a Little Rock municipal court. With neither Baxter nor his attorneys present—nor aware of what was taking place—the inferior court suddenly declared Brooks governor. With a small force of armed supporters, Brooks marched to the Old State House with the court order, forcibly evicted Baxter, and began to fortify the building. Baxter set up headquarters a few blocks east on Markham.

Within hours, thousands had rallied to both sides, with the lion's share of support going to Arkansas native Baxter. Federal troops from the Little Rock Arsenal set up barricades between the opposing forces to prevent violence. Tensions ran high. The Baxter forces dug up an old Civil War cannon, buried during the retreat from Little Rock, and trained it on the Old State House, its threat muted by garlands of flowers strewn upon it by the ladies of the town. But the farce did not prevent bloodshed, and some two hundred persons died in skirmishes fought around the state.[46]

The events in Arkansas created a dilemma for the scandal-ridden administration of President Ulysses S. Grant. If Grant validated Brooks' claim, it would call into question the election results throughout the Reconstructed South. But due process would not allow him to uphold the verdict of a municipal judge over that of the Arkansas Supreme Court. Moreover, the Reconstruction Constitution made the Arkansas legislature the clear arbiter of disputed elections, and the Baxter forces now held a clear majority there. More importantly, support of the American public for Radical Reconstruction was on the ebb, and the Radicals' strength was waning in Congress.

Baxter forced Grant's hand by calling a special session of the legislature to decide the issue. Baxter won, and Grant either had to agree to abide by the decision or be seen as imposing an unpopular government on the people of Arkansas. Baxter's first act upon regaining power was to call for another constitutional convention, which dismantled once and for all the machinery of Reconstruction. Reconstruction was over.[47]

Violence still haunted Arkansawyers, however. Jesse and Frank James robbed the mail north of Harrison in 1870, and Henry Starr robbed the bank in Bentonville in 1893.[48] Arkansas' isolation, rugged terrain, and location adjoining the Indian Territory contributed to lawlessness and gave rise to one of the most unique courts in America.[49] As Reconstruction drew to a close, Federal Judge Isaac C. Parker at Fort Smith and his fierce deputy marshals (immortalized by John Wayne, who earned his only Academy Award as Marshal Rooster Cogburn in the epic *True Grit*) brought law to the area, and Parker became known as the "hanging judge." In the early years there was no appeal from his decisions, which became final when rendered and were followed within days—sometimes only hours—by execution.

RACE RELATIONS IN POST-RECONSTRUCTION ARKANSAS

For a time after Reconstruction, Arkansas held the reputation as a place of economic and political opportunities for blacks.[50] When Augustus H. Garland and the group known as "The Redeemers" came to power following Reconstruction, they took pains to involve blacks in the political process.[51] They did so partly out of a sense of obligation, since many blacks had supported Baxter in his struggle with Brooks. More importantly, Garland—an extraordinary statesman both as a former member of the Confederate Senate and later as U.S. Attorney General in the administration of Grover Cleveland[52]—believed an influx of northern capital was crucial for Arkansas' economic survival and that obtaining capital was impossible in a climate of political and racial violence. Blacks maintained considerable representation in the state legislature and often shared with whites other available political offices.

Pine Bluff was a prime example of the system in action. Among the town's more prominent black citizens was Wiley Jones, who owned the city's streetcar lines.[53] In North Little Rock, a

M.W. Gibbs, elected in 1872 as the first black municipal judge in the U.S.

leading dentist was a black man, and in several other Arkansas towns, prominent black professionals enjoyed a sizable white clientele.[54] Little Rock was an enlightened place in the South and its integrated neighborhoods allowed famed black composer William Grant Still to grow up as an "American boy in an American community."[55]

Arkansas' relative racial moderation made it a mecca for educated blacks from around the country. Among them were men like the remarkable Mifflin W. Gibbs,[56] a free man who made his fortune as a merchant during the California gold rush and then built one of the first railroads in British Columbia. Following these successes, Gibbs studied law and came to Little Rock to establish his practice. He became the first black municipal judge in the United States and later became a U.S. ambassador in Africa. The success of the black middle class was such that the leading black newspaper of the day labeled Arkansas "the Negro Paradise."[57]

Rebuilding the Arkansas Economy

Arkansas counted on a resurgence of agriculture to heal the ravages of war. Many of Arkansas' pre-war planters still held land, but had virtually no cash with which to make a crop. Many were forced to sell off parts of their estates to meet taxes or buy seed and supplies. This depressed the price of land and made it almost worthless as collateral. Since northerners had access to cash, they made significant inroads into Arkansas' planter population. But soon their capital, too, was depleted, and they felt the same pinch as their neighbors. The only people willing to lend were the cotton brokers, and the only security they would accept was future crops. This "crop lien" was available only on cotton. Moreover, because of overproduction, as well as federal currency and tariff policies, cotton prices were entering a cycle of recession and depression that would persist well into the next century.

Unable to pay for the labor of ex-slaves when cash was such a precious commodity, planters developed a system which mirrored the exploitative relationship they suffered at the hands of the cotton brokers: sharecropping.[58] Planters leased land to ex-slaves and furnished them supplies on credit to be paid by a share of the future crop. For the freedmen, it amounted to a virtual reinstitution of slavery. Each year the tenant found himself deeper in debt, unable to leave the land for fear of imprisonment for reneging on his contract.

For the poor white owners of small farms, the situation was similar. Even in the highlands, the only credit available was a crop lien. This led to the ludicrous practice of growing so-called "shoe-top" cotton on unsuitable land. The practice was particularly pronounced in the foothills bordering the delta. Many farmers found themselves caught in a spiral of debt that was steadily reducing them to the status of sharecroppers.

The plight of Arkansas farmers gave rise to one of the early grass roots agrarian movements in America—the Agricultural Wheel.[59] Remarkably, the Wheel was bi-racial, including many black chapters among its ranks. At first, the Wheel was primarily a self-help organization for farmers. It urged self-reliance, preached avoidance of one-crop agriculture, and warned its members against the evils of the crop lien. Soon, however, the Wheel came to realize that many of the issues facing farmers required legislation, such as currency reform, taxes for rural roads, election reform, a change in the usury laws, and regulation of the railroads. To influence such legislation required political power, and their quest for power culminated in the election of 1888.[60]

There seems little doubt the agrarian forces captured the reins of state government in 1888 only to have this victory stolen in perhaps the most corrupt election in Arkansas history. A subsequent merger with the all-white Farmer's Union robbed the Wheel of its political energy, and changes in the state election laws in 1891 eliminated blacks as a coherent political force until after World War II.[61]

Ironically, the 1891 election law appears to have been genuinely intended as a reform; its primary purpose was to end the sort of corruption prevalent in 1888. As it turned out, the parts of the bill that would prove the most damaging to the black vote were precisely the sorts of measures hailed as progressive reforms to stop corruption of New York's Tammany Hall and elsewhere in the country. The key provisions were a prohibition on campaigning near the polls and the institution of the Australian, or secret, ballot.

Because many black voters were illiterate and had reason to fear intimidation from landlords and employers, it was the practice of black precinct captains to hold rallies or barbecues on election day to distribute pre-marked ballots and then march the voters en masse to the polls. The new law outlawed such marches and banned pre-marked ballots. If the voter was illiterate or otherwise had trouble marking his ballot, he had to ask the election judges for assistance. Denied the safety of numbers and faced with the prospect of a humiliating ordeal and the chance of retribution, black voters stayed away in droves during the 1892 election. Coupled with the dollar poll tax, ostensibly required to verify voter residency requirements, poor white and black voters alike were eliminated, and Republicans, blacks, and agrarian reformers were swept out of office. The old power sharing arrangements were abandoned.

Many educated blacks deserted Arkansas for the North and West.[62] Hundreds of black farmers left for the newly opened Oklahoma Territory. Arkansas also became one of the leading centers of the Back-to-Africa Movement, and hundreds left the state to help found a new colony in Liberia, on the west Africa coast.

THE RAILROAD

Although Republicans had bankrupted the treasury in an attempt to push railroads forward during Reconstruction, they were right about one thing: railroads were the key to Arkansas' development. Construction had begun before the Civil War, but the real boom came in the 1880s when the state's mileage more than tripled as the empires of Jay Gould and others linked up across Arkansas.[63]

Most Arkansawyers had a love-hate relationship with the railroad, with hot political controversies revolving around

railroad taxation and regulation, but the real grudge held against
the railroads was that they helped make Arkansawyers the
laughing stock of the nation. A less-than-altogether-successful
brakeman known as Three-Finger Jackson published a book
containing a collection of drummer and minstrel stories he had
heard during his years of railroading in the Ozarks. His book, *On
a Slow Train Through Arkansas*, maligned the state. No one would
have paid it much mind, except that Jackson convinced the
railroads it was the perfect thing to read on the train. The book
was sold in just about every depot in America. It went through so
many printings that it was the best-selling copyrighted book of all
time until *Gone With the Wind* came along.[64]

For all that, the railroads were a blessing. They ended the
centuries-long economic and geographic isolation of Arkansas.
The major routes crossed near the capitol. One, the present-day
Union Pacific, followed the Southwest Trail, traversing Arkansas
diagonally on a route from St. Louis to Texas. The Southwest
Trail had originally been used by Indians, as it skirted the Ozark
and Ouachita Mountains. This same route is now part of the
federal highway system. Another route bisecting Arkansas from
Memphis to Fort Smith would later become the route of the
famed Rock Island Rockets. A spur connecting the two turned
the Old State House around when it cut off access to the front
entrance on the north side, thereby causing the present front
entrance to be constructed on the south side of the building. One
of many routes which did not pass near the capitol deserves
special mention, since the cotton fields of Arkansas gave it
identity: the Cotton Belt Route of the former Southern Pacific.
In all there would be over ninety railroads in Arkansas by the
outbreak of World War I.[65]

Many railroads advertised for sale Arkansas lands that had
been part of federal grants to the railroads to encourage their
construction. For example, in response to a solicitation by the

Little Rock and Fort Smith Railroad Land Office,[66] a nineteenth-century freedom fighter, Count Timothy Von Choinski, led three hundred Polish settlers to the Marche community just a few miles from the capitol site. The St. Louis and Iron Mountain Railroad advertised Arkansas lands for sale, saying, "men wanted for good homes, cheap lands, in a genial climate, near good markets, in fine country, with good people" and with additional claims such

Get a Home in Arkansas

✳ ✳ ✳

The Land of Fruits, Good Health and Plenty.

Two Million Acres .....

⚜ FINE FARMING, GRAZING, TIMBERED, FRUIT AND MINERAL LANDS, IN TRACTS TO SUIT PURCHASERS.

Mild Climate, Low Prices, Easy Payments, Varied Products, Low Interest.

G. A. A. DEANE, Land Commissioner, Little Rock, Ark.

Advertisement for land in Arkansas, circa 1895.

as "Arkansas has probably the finest variety of valuable timber to be found in the United States accessible to market," and "These rich bottoms are as productive as the Delta of Egypt."[67]

The railroad provided a way to get goods to market. It made possible the fruit industry of north Arkansas; it opened the hill country to mining; the entire state to lumbering; and made it possible for tourists to get conveniently to mountain spas like Hot Springs and Eureka Springs.

ARKANSAS INDUSTRY

Mining was a true bonanza, for the geology of Arkansas is one of the most remarkable in the world. Besides oil and gas, it contains an unusual array of minerals, including silver, copper, lead, manganese, coal, lignite, iron, kaolin, zinc, novaculite, the nation's largest bauxite deposits, and the nation's only diamond mine.[68]

Though the exploitation of Ozark hardwood began much earlier, Arkansas' real lumber boom came early in the twentieth century, when the railroads breached the state's final wilderness: the sparsely populated Ouachita Mountains. The cutting of this last great virgin forest east of the Rocky Mountains provided a new livelihood and lifestyle for Arkansawyers, but analysis of the logging and mining industry reflects a pattern that would become typical for much of Arkansas' economy.

Originally many saw mills and mines were locally owned, but over the years the extraction of forest products and minerals became the province of outside interests. With low taxes on land and plenty of natural resources, the principal benefit to Arkansawyers has been the payment of wages, not the accumulation of capital or investment in public improvements. Today, almost two-thirds of Arkansas manufacturing is owned by non-resident companies,[69] but there are notable exceptions in several sectors. Tyson Foods, the nation's largest poultry processor, is headquartered in Springdale; Stuttgart is home to Riceland, the nation's largest rice miller; Anderson's Minnow Farm, headquartered in Lonoke, is the world's largest; Little Rock's TCBY is the nation's largest soft-serve frozen yogurt company; Wal-Mart, the nation's largest retailer, is headquartered in Bentonville; Dillard's, another national retailing chain, is headquartered in Little Rock; and Stephens Inc., headquartered in Little Rock, was once the nation's largest investment banker located outside Wall Street.

Tourism has historically been an important source of both capital and employment, and thousands of tourists flocked to the medicinal springs and scenic terrain of Hot Springs once the railroads linked the town with the outside

Advertisement for Arkansas tourism, circa 1926.

world. As far back as 1832, Hot Springs had been the first public land in the United States to be set aside for protection by the federal government and ultimately became the nation's only urban national park.[70]

Hot Springs' success provoked a veritable land rush when similar mineral waters were discovered at Eureka Springs, but the two resorts were very different in character. Since its inception, Hot Springs has boasted a race track, crystal merchants, alligator and ostrich farms, casinos, and bordellos in addition to its healing baths. It was the site of major league baseball's first spring training camp. Its "anything goes" reputation survived for nearly a century, and during Prohibition, Hot Springs was a "truce" town where gangsters like Al Capone could vacation.[71] Eureka Springs, on the other hand, was much more genteel, with its winding streets lined with Victorian gingerbread houses. Its immense Crescent Hotel was heralded as the most luxurious resort hotel in America in 1886.[72] While genteel in some respects, temperance activist Carrie Nation's Hatchet Hall is also located in Eureka Springs.[73]

The late nineteenth and early twentieth centuries were the golden age of Arkansas boosterism. Convinced that Arkansas' poor national image hampered the state in its efforts to attract industry, the business and political leaders of the day sought to accentuate the positive and eliminate the negative, employing every conceivable means at their disposal—from lecture tours to promotional trains complete with miniature rice fields; from elaborate exhibits at the 1876 Centennial Exposition and the 1939 World's Fair to promotional songs, banners, buttons, postcards, and letter-writing campaigns.

The state was making remarkable strides on many fronts: public health, prison reform, education, road construction, tax reform—even railroad regulation.[74] The state Democratic Party was one of the first in the South to allow women to vote in its primaries, and Arkansas was among the first to ratify the amendment granting women's suffrage. State government outgrew the confines of the Old State House and a grand new state capitol was occupied in 1911.

ACHIEVEMENTS IN SCIENCE

A story within a story is the Old State House's role in medicine resulting from construction of the present capitol.[75] Arkansas physicians had struggled since statehood to obtain licensing of physicians and public support for medical education. On the frontier, medical practitioners fell into three groups: allopaths who practiced blood-letting, blistering, and other accepted nineteenth-century practices; botanic or "Indian"

The Old State House, circa 1960.

doctors who used herbs and brandy therapy; and homeopaths, who, in the German tradition, administered minimal drugs if at all. Not until 1903 did the state finally establish a board to license physicians, and not until 1909 was a diploma from a recognized medical school required to practice medicine. The reluctance to license physicians and require formal education to practice medicine closely paralleled Arkansas' rural suspicion of education during the period, for, as the second president of the Arkansas Medical Society declared, "the most ignorant...mountebank can...practice medicine...because the public...are themselves ignorant."[76]

With the support of the Arkansas Medical Society, which was formed at the close of the Civil War, a private for-profit company formed a medical school in 1879, which became accepted as the Medical Department of the University of Arkansas on condition that the state assume no financial responsibility. Finally, in 1912, the state appropriated funds for the medical school and gave it the recently vacated Old State House for a building, where it remained, cadavers and all, until 1935.[77]

Thus the Old State House fostered numerous American achievements in medicine by Arkansas physicians and scientists including the discovery of effective treatment of tuberculosis; a pioneering "bone stretching" cure for slow bone growth; the discovery of Vitamin M; pioneering laser treatment of cancer of the head and neck; pioneering removal of birthmarks by laser surgery; the discovery that anemia resulted from Vitamin E deficiency; original research on the reaction of body tissue to suture materials; the publication of the textbook classic on radiology; the development of a special surgical needle; the introduction of laser treatment to improve circulation in blood vessels of the elderly; and incunabula research of organ transplants. It was the third hospital in the world to crush kidney stones without anesthesia. It established an environment for achievement in Arkansas medicine. Today, Arkansas Children's Hospital, which borders the state capitol grounds, is yet another example of Arkansas' medical achievements—it is one of the top ten children's hospitals in the nation, with patients from all over the world.[78]

PROGRESS IN THE EARLY TWENTIETH CENTURY

The turn of the century was a time of tremendous progress and change, but also one of enduring values. The farmers, lumbermen, miners—the overwhelming majority of Arkansawyers—still owed their livelihood to the land's bounty. The early twentieth century generation of Arkansawyers learned that nature's gifts could not be taken for granted. Waste and greed squandered much of the petroleum and natural gas resources. Forests were clear-cut and abandoned. Farm lands were

The black-owned Black Diamond Drug Store in Helena, circa 1910.

plagued by flood, drought, erosion, and illiterate farmers. According to a recent agriculture publication, Arkansas agriculture today "is among the most efficient in the world."[79] In 1900, however, the tenant farmer's average livestock holding was one mule, three hogs, six chickens, and no cow, and he and his family were destined to poverty in the grasp of King Cotton.

The anti-intellectual Populist attitude did not fade easily. Notwithstanding Governor Archibald Yell's 1842 request for agricultural research funds, scientific agriculture did not materialize until after the Civil War, when New York,

Connecticut, and other eastern states, fearing competition from plains and southern farmers, supported federal legislation for establishing agriculture experiment stations. The one established in Fayetteville in 1888 was situated in the northwest Arkansas mountains, far from the delta cotton fields, but scientists such as the first director, Albert E. Menke, slowly began educating farmers on the value of crop rotation, contour plowing, and crop diversification from cotton to rice, oats, fruits, vegetables, cattle, and poultry, which helped lead to today's efficiency.[80]

Results were impressive, for as early as 1919, fruit production had made the apple cider vinegar plant in Rogers the largest in the world,[81] and strawberries boosted the White County economy in 1929 to the extent that it had more paved roads than the entire state of Montana.[82] The state was the site of the earliest experiments in reforestation.[83] Restrictions were even placed on hunting and fishing. Such conservation was a remarkable change in attitude toward resources once thought limitless.[84]

WORLD WAR I AND THE DEPRESSION

Change came quickly in the next generation as well. World War I devoured Arkansas minerals and resources, especially cotton. Eberts Field in Lonoke, carved out of cotton fields, was the second largest air training field in the country.[85] For a time, war brought prosperity to Arkansas,[86] but the armistice in 1918 was followed by a collapse of cotton prices. Thus more and more white farmers were driven by bankruptcy into the ranks of sharecroppers, and racial violence, seen elsewhere in the cotton belt, erupted in the repression of black citizens, contributing to the Elaine race riots in 1919.[87] Ironically, this tragic confrontation produced one of the great milestones of American constitutional law, when Arkansas lawyer Scipio A. Jones, the black son of a slave who "read law" to become licensed to practice, convinced the United States

Supreme Court to authorize for the first time federal court *habeas corpus* review of state court decisions, thereby overturning the death sentences of twelve men who had been denied a fair trial.[88]

Then came the Great Depression, which began a decade early in Arkansas with the collapse of cotton prices.[89] The calamity was compounded in 1927 by a disastrous flood on the Mississippi and its tributaries, inundating over five million acres, or an eighth of the state.[90] Then came drought. The cumulative effect was devastating to the Arkansas economy, and the first to suffer were the sharecroppers and farm laborers. A protest by hungry farmers in England, Arkansas, gained national attention, as did the efforts of the Southern Tenant Farmers Union,[91] a multi-racial sharecropper organization founded in the Arkansas delta. These events in Arkansas had a dramatic impact on shaping the farm relief policies of President Roosevelt's New Deal, and a significant milestone was construction near Greenbrier of the nation's first watershed project by the Soil Conservation Service.

The Depression also brought a revival of the old populist philosophy. Arkansas has always tended to elect populist candidates, with Jeff Davis and Orval Faubus among the more notable. But electing the first woman in American history to the United States Senate is perhaps the most significant event of national politics in twentieth-century Arkansas until the Clinton era.[92]

Hattie Caraway was appointed to serve the remainder of her husband's Senate term after his death. She surprised many when she ran for a full term, and the 1932 election proved to be one of the turning points in Arkansas history. She was assisted in that quest by her Senate seat mate, Huey P. Long, the Louisiana "Kingfish." Arkansas was in the throes of the Great Depression, Hitler was talking about the "fatherland" in Germany, and the state experienced a political campaign that would affect Arkansas politics for generations. In just seven days, Hattie,

Long, and a seven vehicle caravan—including sound trucks and truckloads of chairs, water, and campaign material—stormed through Arkansas. Voters heard the message of the "haves" versus the "have nots" and listened to the demure Senator Caraway's persistent attacks on federal agencies that gave relief to banks and railroads but not to simple folks. The flamboyant Long, dressed in a white suit, pink shirt, green tie, and black and white shoes, quoted scripture and prayed for the soldier's bonus and "this little lady." Nearly twenty-five thousand people heard speeches in five south Arkansas rallies the first day. One week later Hattie had almost more votes than all four of her opponents combined.

It was populism at its best.

WORLD WAR II

World War II finally brought an end to the Great Depression in Arkansas.[93] Several of the nation's war industries and military facilities were located in the state—ammunition plants at Camden, Maumelle, and Jacksonville; an arsenal at Pine Bluff; five air fields; and two major training camps, one at Fort Chaffee near Fort Smith and another at Camp Robinson outside North Little Rock, where artillery fire once again rattled the windows of the capitol building. Most of the Allies' aluminum was processed from Arkansas bauxite mined just a few miles from the capitol.[94]

Two war facilities, however, were sad chapters in American history. Almost nineteen thousand Japanese-Americans were relocated to internment camps at Rohwer and Jerome in the southeast Arkansas delta. Many of these west coast citizens got a glimpse of the state capitol as they were transported by train to endure the war years behind barbed wire in cheerless barracks and difficult climate, simply because of fear and outrage over America's early losses at Pearl Harbor.[95]

Even though the United States' military was segregated, Little Rock's Ottenheimer brothers became the first employers in the South to employ blacks in factory production lines. Otherwise, Arkansas' home front during World War II mirrored the rest of America's: paper drives, contribution of clothes for war victims, and victory gardens.

Although near the bottom in per capita income, long lines of Arkansas patriots formed to purchase war bonds at a sky-rocketing rate so successful that some sales drew *Life* magazine and other national media attention.[96] Women entered the work force, running machinery and managing farms and businesses. Midway through the war, twenty percent of the industrial work force in Arkansas were women, and by the end of the war the men's work/women's work distinction had changed forever.[97]

Minuteman statue at Camp Robinson's National Guard Professional Education Center, the nation's school for technical education of the National Guard forces, now located where thousands of Americans trained during World Wars I and II.

Even women's fashions changed permanently as blue jeans and slacks on the assembly line replaced skirts and dresses.

As the tide of war changed, it became a great source of pride that Fort Smith's Bill Darby led the famed Darby's Rangers; that one of history's great generals, Douglas MacArthur, was born at the U.S. Army Arsenal across town from the state capitol; and that Monticello native John Shirley Wood became known as the Rommel of the American armed forces. General Patton said Wood's accomplishments "have never been equaled...in the history of warfare."[98]

One of the most far-reaching acts of the Arkansas legislature was passed in the last year of World War II: the Revenue Stabilization Act.[99] This law required the state to live within its means (its current revenues) and forbade deficit spending other than through bond issues. As recently as the late 1980s, the law was hailed as a model for reducing the federal deficit.

Arkansas' long-delayed industrialization began in earnest during World War II.[100] The late start forestalled a single-industry state, and today Arkansas' economy has great diversity. For example, at the close of the twentieth century, there are thirty-six manufacturing plants in Arkansas employing more than a thousand people. Arkansas-made products include data communication equipment; sporting ammunition; vegetable, grain, and poultry processing; laser equipment; parking meters; caviar; electric motors; appliance motors; air-to-air missiles; refrigerators; freezers; small arms; watches; heating and air conditioning equipment; paper; munitions; plywood; news print; microwave ovens; greeting cards; rubber tires; cosmetics; chemicals; medical equipment; aircraft components; furniture; leather goods; and apparel.[101]

THE CENTRAL HIGH CRISIS

Just as progress in the era of boosterism gave way to the Great Depression, the progress of the postwar era gave way to Arkansas' old nemeses: race relations and self-image. Both were dealt severe setbacks in unquestionably the most dramatic chapter of the state's postwar history, the event that marked the coming of age of television journalism—Governor Faubus' mobilization of the National Guard to prevent the integration of Little Rock Central High School in 1957-58. Central High was the first great televised event of the civil rights movement, one which marred the perception of Arkansas for generations of Americans with images of bayonets, even though there were no hospitalized injuries or deaths.[102] Ironically, ten years earlier Arkansas had made significant progress in integrating education, having become the first medical school in the South to admit blacks.[103] Another irony is that the events at Central High resulted in little actual violence, much less than in subsequent incidents throughout the South, California's Watts, and northern cities such as Chicago, Boston, Baltimore, and New York. What few people realize is that the Little Rock desegregation process was part of a voluntary plan undertaken by the Little Rock School Board[104] after uneventful integration of other Arkansas schools. Had they waited for a federal court order, they might have avoided entirely the stigma of being first, and the loss of a whole school year when the schools were closed. In response, Mrs. D.D. Terry, sitting under a portrait of her father in his Confederate uniform, joined forces with Mrs. Joe R. Brewer and Mrs. J.O. Powell to form the Women's Emergency Committee to Open our Schools, "the first group of white women in the South to champion public education."[105]

Today, Central High is a National Governor's Association Model School teaching Greek, Latin, and twenty-first century sciences to all races. Each year during the 1980s, Central alone produced ten percent or more of Arkansas' National Merit Scholars, and its high academic standing is widely recognized by college admission offices throughout America.

THE ROAD TO THE TWENTY-FIRST CENTURY

Many credit Winthrop Rockefeller with building Arkansas in spite of the Central High crisis. As the grandson of one of America's industrial giants, John D. Rockefeller, he was ideally suited to head the Arkansas Industrial Development Commission. Later as governor, he championed government and social reform that made the state more attractive to business. By 1980, Arkansas' population had shifted from rural to urban.[106] Even so, the economy is still heavily agricultural, and the state ranks first in the nation in chicken and rice production, and in the top ten in cotton, eggs, grapes, grain sorghum, pecans, snap beans, soybeans, tomatoes, and turkeys. As Arkansas became more urban, the "colonial" idea of cheap wages faded. Today, for example, scientific laboratories employ approximately one hundred research scientists at the National Center for Toxicological Research, which is just downriver from the state capitol in Jefferson County.

For well over a century Arkansas has striven to change its basic economic structure from economic colonialism to vigorous, full-fledged capitalism. Today, Arkansas is still very much a part of the Deep South, where magnolias and azaleas grow, alligators swim, and the Chevrolet pickup is the most common vehicle.[107] At the same time, Arkansas is part of the Southwest, where cactus spread, armadillos and roadrunners scurry, and the nuclear power plant at London, Arkansas is the first built in the Southwest. Like the other Sunbelt residents, Arkansawyers look to the future with reliance on the state's old values. And

Arkansas' values are solid: its natural resources, its traditions, and its people.

From border to border, Arkansas industry leads in many diverse fields. In southwest Arkansas, Ashdown's Nekoosa Papers Plant is the largest fine grade paper mill in the world, and in northeast Arkansas, Blytheville's Nucor-Yamaha Steel Mill is the most technologically advanced mini-mill found anywhere. Arkansas' top ten private employers are Emerson Electric, Georgia Pacific Corporation, Whirlpool, ConAgra, International Paper Company, Baldor Electric, White Consolidated Industries (Frigidaire and Poulan), American Greetings Corporation, Tyson Foods, and Wal-Mart. The international character of Arkansas business is mirrored by

The historic Pulaski County Courthouse against the background of the Stephens Building, home of Stephens Inc., once the nation's largest investment banking firm located outside New York City's Wall Street.

two of its international charities: Heifer Project International in Little Rock, with activities in thirty-eight countries, and Winrock International on Petit Jean Mountain, with projects in thirty-four countries. Another significant segment is Arkansas' tourism industry, which is one-fourth the size of the manufacturing industry in terms of employment.[108]

Perhaps Arkansas' greatest natural resource today is water. From the world-famous Mountain Valley Water Company at Hot Springs to the state's vast river system, which carries 280 billion gallons of water every day,[109] Arkansas' water holds unlimited promise. In contrast to its nineteenth-century use for transportation, Arkansas' water in the twenty-first century will be the backbone for agriculture, industry, and health. Typically, the capitol is served by a municipal water system from mountain lake resources that are projected to be adequate until the year 2070.

The traditions of old-time religion and old-fashioned patriotism helped Arkansas through trying years, and in most communities today, churches are still the centers of social life, with events such as pie suppers, picnics, church socials, baptisms, and camp meetings still commonplace, even in an internet society. And the Arkansas spirit still blazes new trails, for in 1983 the Arkansas Conference of Churches and Synagogues became the first major statewide inter-faith organization in America.[110] In 1996, Arkansas people led the nation in philanthropy, ranking number one in the generosity index of *The Chronicle of Philanthropy*.[111]

Even Arkansas' meals have a great—and lasting—tradition. Arkansas feasts of wild duck with rice, seafood sausage, fried catfish, and sweet potato pie can trace their lineage to earlier victuals such as cracklin' bread, poke "sallet," watermelon rind preserves, and fruit leather.

The tradition of living with nature and working near home hasn't changed now that the majority of Arkansawyers live in municipalities. Most commute in less than fifteen minutes, and there's still plenty of room to hunt and fish and breathe.

Arkansas' tradition is also seen in today's heritage of historic names: Lavaca, L'Anguille, Hiwasse, Bayou Meto, Prague, and London reflect a rich diversity of people.[112] Indeed, Arkansas' history, its future, and its greatness are the Arkansas people. Davy Crockett said it for posterity in the winter before statehood: "If I could rest anywhere, it would be in Arkansaw, where men are of the real half-horse, half-alligator breed such as grows nowhere else on the universal earth."[113] From the earliest Quapaw to the latest Arkansas traveler, the men and women of Arkansas are unique. They have built a state on a remarkable tradition of self reliance, hard work, and savvy that sets the pace for today's Arkansawyers, whose capitol building now sits at the crossroads of the future.

Street sign at Wilkiewicz and Szymanski Roads in northern Pulaski County, Arkansas.

NOTES

1. Morse, Dan F. *Sloan: A Paleo Indian Dalton Cemetery*. Washington, D.C.: Smithsonian Institution Press, 1997, p. xv.

2. McGimsey III, Charles K. *Indians of Arkansas*. Fayetteville: Arkansas Archeological Survey, 1969, pp. 22 and 28-29.

3. Baird, W. David. *The Quapaws*. New York: Chelsea House, 1989, p. 14.

4. Arnold, Judge Morris S. *Colonial Arkansas 1686-1804*. Fayetteville: University of Arkansas Press, 1991. Records Arkansas' complex colonial history.

5. Ferguson, John L., and J.H. Atkinson. *Historic Arkansas*. Little Rock: Arkansas History Commission, 1983, pp. 8-12.

6. *ibid*. pp. 14-15.

7. Hempstead, Fay. *Historical Review of Arkansas: Its Commerce, Industry and Modern Affairs*. Vol.1. Chicago: The Lewis Publishing Company, 1911, pp. 5-8.

8. Ashmore, Harry S. *Arkansas: A Bicentennial History*. New York: W.W. Norton & Co. Inc., 1978, p. 7.

9. Whayne, Jeannie. *Cultural Encounters in the Early South: Indians and Europeans in Arkansas*. Fayetteville: University of Arkansas Press, 1995, pp. 89-91.

10. *ibid*. pp. 129-130.

11. Dougan, Michael B. *Arkansas Odyssey: The Saga of Arkansas from Prehistoric Times to Present*. Little Rock: Rose Publishing Co., Inc., 1994, p. 66.

12. *ibid*. p. 108.

13. Dougan, p. 122-123.

14. Ross, Margaret. *Arkansas Gazette: The Early Years*. Chicago: Lakeside Press, 1969, pp. 122-123.

15. Hempstead, p. 58-59.

16. Bearss, Edwin C. "In Quest of Peace on the Indian Border." *Arkansas Historical Quarterly*, Vol. 23, 1964, p. 136.

17. Lester, Jim, and Judy Lester. *Greater Little Rock*. Norfolk, Va.: Donning Company Publishers, 1986, p. 23.

18. Dougan, pp. 133, 136.

19. Paulson, Allen C. *Roadside History of Arkansas*. Missoula, Mont.: Mountain Press Publishing Company, 1998, pp. 198-200.

20. Dougan, p. 80.

21. *ibid*. p. 79.

22. *ibid*. pp. 73-75.

23. *ibid*. pp. 76-80.

24. For excellent descriptions of the country store, see Thomas D. Clark, *Pills, Petticoats, and Plows: The Southern Country Store* (Indianapolis: Bobbs-Merrill Co., 1944).

25. Paulson, p. 177.

26. Dougan, p. 100.

27. *ibid*. pp. 160-161.

28. Donovan, Timothy P. et al, eds. *The Governors of Arkansas: Essays in Political Biography*. Fayetteville: University of Arkansas Press, 1995, pp. 33-35.

29. Fletcher, John Gould. *Arkansas*. Fayetteville: University of Arkansas Press, 1989, p. 121.

30. Thompson, George H. *Arkansas and Reconstruction: The Influence of Geography, Economics and Personality*. New York: Kennikat Press Corp., 1976, pp. 20, 21.

31. Thomas, David Y. *Arkansas in War and Reconstruction.* Little Rock: Central Printing Company, 1926, p. 92. Also John L. Ferguson. *Arkansas and the Civil War.* Little Rock: Pioneer Press, 1962, p. 321.

32. Fessler, Paul R. "The Case of the Missing Promotion: Historians and the Military Career of Major General Patrick Ronayne Clayburne, C.S.A." *Arkansas Historical Quarterly,* Vol. 53, 1994, p. 211.

33. Christ, Mark K. *Rugged and Sublime.* Fayetteville: University of Arkansas Press, 1994, pp. 92-94.

34. Earngey, Bill. *Arkansas Roadsides.* Little Rock: East Mountain Press, 1987, p. 89.

35. Christ, pp. 110-128.

36. *ibid.* pp. 42, 163.

37. *Arkansas Times, A History of Arkansas.* Little Rock: Arkansas Writer's Project, Inc., 1994, pp. 80-84.

38. Franks, Kenny A. *Stan Watie.* Memphis, Tenn.: Memphis State University Press, 1979, p. 181.

39. Paulson, p. 6.

40. Fletcher, pp. 153-155.

41. Smith, John I. *The Courage of a Southern Unionist.* Little Rock: Rose Publishing Company, 1979, p. 64.

42. Donovan, Timothy P., William B. Gatewood, Jr., Jeannie M. Whayne, eds. *The Governors of Arkansas: Essays in Political Biography.* Fayetteville: University of Arkansas Press, 2d ed., 1995, pp. 46-57.

43. Ferguson and Atkinson, pp. 156-158.

44. Thompson, p. 101.

45. Fletcher, pp. 194-219.

46. Dougan, p. 262.

47. Fletcher, p. 220.

48. Paulson, p. 325.

49. Ashmore, pp. 163-164.

50. Gordon, Fon Louise. *Caste and Class: The Black Experience in Arkansas, 1880-1920.* Athens, Ga.: University of Georgia Press, 1995, p. 10.

51. *ibid.*

52. Dougan, p. 269.

53. *ibid.* pp. 316.

54. Graves, John W. *Town and Country: Race Relations in an Urban-Rural Context, Arkansas, 1865-1905.* Fayetteville: University of Arkansas Press, 1990, pp. 97-133.

55. Arvey, Verna. *In One Lifetime.* Fayetteville: University of Arkansas Press, 1984, pp. 13-16.

56. Herndon, Dallas T. *Annals of Arkansas.* Hopkinsville, Ky.: Historical Records Ass'n., Vol. 1, 1947, p. 451.

57. Graves. *supra.*

58. Fletcher, pp. 278-293.

59. Dougan, pp. 302-304.

60. Ashmore, pp. 128-131.

61. *Arkansas Times*, p. 104.

62. Gordon, p. 122.

63. Dougan, p. 282.

64. *ibid.* pp. 543-544.

65. Hull, Clifton E. *Shortline Railroads of Arkansas.* Norman, Okla.: University of Oklahoma Press, 1969, p. 399. Also, Hanson, G.T., and C.H. Moneyhon. *Historical Atlas of Arkansas.* Norman, Okla.: University of Oklahoma Press, 1989, p. 49.

66.Besancon-Alford, Julia G. "The History of Marche, Arkansas," *Pulaski County Historical Review.* Vol. XLI (Winter 1993), pp. 78-90.

67. Iron Mountain & Southern Railway Co. *Map of the Arkansas Land Grants.* St. Louis: Globe Democrat, ca. 1900.

68. Smith, Richard M. *The Atlas of Arkansas.* Fayetteville: University of Arkansas Press, 1989, p. 161. Also Owen, David

Dale. *Geological Reconnaissance of Arkansas*. Little Rock: C. Sherman & Son, 1860, p. 9.

69. Smith, p. 170.

70. *ibid.* p. 196.

71. Today the plaque on Room 443 of Hot Springs' Arlington Hotel identifies the "Al Capone Suite."

72. Paulson, p. 331.

73. Dougan, p. 345.

74. Ferguson and Atkinson, pp. 257-262, 277, 278.

75. See generally, W. David Baird, *Medical Education in Arkansas 1879-1978* (Memphis, Tenn.: Memphis State University Press, 1979).

76. *ibid.* pp. 14, 15.

77. *ibid.* pp. p. 106.

78. Baird, *supra.*

79. Strausberg, Stephen F. *A Century of Research*. Fayetteville: Arkansas Agriculture Experiment Station, 1989, p. 1.

80. *ibid.* pp. 1-32, 79.

81. Paulson, p. 327.

82. *ibid.* pp. 358.

83. Strausberg, p. 87.

84. Patterson, Gregg. "The Age of Exploitation: 1915-1944," *Arkansas Game and Fish Magazine*. Vol. 17 (May/June 1986), pp. 15-22.

85. Paulson, p. 54.

86. Ashmore, pp. 164-165.

87. Ferguson and Atkisson, p. 274.

88. *Moore v. Dempsey*, 261 U.S. 86 (1923).

89. Dougan, p. 387.

90. Daniel, Pete. *Deep'n as It Come*. Fayetteville: University of Arkansas Press, 1996, p. 7.

91. Fletcher, pp. 286-287.

92. Malone, David. *Hattie and Huey*. Fayetteville: University of Arkansas Press, 1986, pp. xi-xiii.

93. Ferguson and Atkinson, p. 301.

94. Smith, C. Calvin. *War and Wartime Changes: The Transformation of Arkansas 1940-1945*. Fayetteville: University of Arkansas Press, 1986, pp. 20, 21.

95. *ibid.* pp. 64, 65.

96. *ibid.* pp. 15, 16.

97. *ibid.* p. 31.

98. Sallee, Bob. "Arkansan often overlooked in WWII hero stories," *Arkansas Democrat Gazette* 10 Sept. 1998.

99. Dougan, p. 480.

100. C. Smith, p. 19, 20.

101. R. Smith, pp. 173-185.

102. Huckaby, Elizabeth. *Crisis at Central High*. Baton Rouge: Louisiana State University Press, 1980, pp. xi, xii, 42.

103. Baird, p. 211.

104. Dougan, pp. 498-499.

105. Brewer, Vivion. *The Embattled Ladies of Little Rock*. Ft. Bragg, Calif.: Lost Coast Press, 1999, cover.

106. R. Smith, p. 53.

107. Author's interview with Fred Porter, Administrator of the Arkansas Office of Motor Vehicles (Sept. 1999).

108. R. Smith, pp. 171, 189.

109. *ibid.* pp. 24, 25.

110. Author's interview with Rev. Bryan Fulwider, President Arkansas Interfaith Conference, (Sept. 1999).

111. Debra E. Blum. "Giving Goes West," *The Chronicle of Philanthropy*, August 27, 1998. pp. 9-13.

112. See Appendix 4 for representative list, and see generally Ernie Dean, *Arkansas Place Names* (Branson, Mo.: The Ozarks Mountaineer, 1986).

113. Paulson, p. 92.

Appendix One

Arkansawyers

Among the Arkansas people who have contributed to our world are:

Bill Fulbright, Senate foreign relations chairman and namesake of the international scholarship
Albert Pike, poet, soldier, and statesman
Joe T. Robinson, 1928 Democratic vice-presidential nominee
Joycelyn Elders, Surgeon General of the United States
General Wesley Clark, NATO Commander
Footsie Britt, the first soldier to win the four top medals for gallantry
Admiral John S. Thatch, naval air tactician
Alford L. McMichael, Sergeant Major of the U.S. Marine Corps
Glen Campbell and **Johnny Cash**, singers
Bill Clinton, President of the United States
Floyd Cramer, pianist
Thase Daniel, premier wildlife photographer
Fred Graham, CBS news correspondent
Fay Jones and **Edward Durrell Stone**, international architects

Tracy Mills, fashion designer
Dick Powell, movie star
Charlotte Stephens, educator
William Grant Still, composer
Lily Peter, poet laureate
Marjorie Lawrence and **Mignon Dunn**, opera greats
John Gould Fletcher, Pulitzer Prize poet
Paul Greenberg, Pulitzer Prize editorial writer
Miller Williams, Prix de Rome poet
I. Denton, woodcarver
Sister Rosetta Thorpe, gospel singer featured on a 1998
    U.S. Postage Stamp
Donna Axum and **Elizabeth Ward Gracen**, Miss Americas
Maya Angelou, poet
Patsy Montana, country singer
Sonny Boy Williamson, bluesman
Sarah Caldwell, New York Metropolitan Opera Conductor
Cyrus Adler, Jewish historian
Al Hibbler, singer
Robert A. Leflar, constitutional scholar
Vance Randolph, folklorist
Justin Tyler Carroll, age fourteen, winner of the 1996 National
    Spelling Bee
Carroll Cloar, prolific artist of the South
C. Vann Woodward, Pulitzer Prize historian
Paul Day and **William Darby**, nutritionists and inventors of
    vitamin M
Bettye Caldwell, child psychologist
M. Gazi Yasargil, neurosurgery "Man of the Century"
John McDonald, Razorback coach, holder of more national
    championships (twenty-eight) than any coach in any sport
    in history
Bear Bryant, the winningest coach in college football

Dizzy Dean, baseball sportscaster
Sidney Moncrief, basketball great
Brooks Robinson, Baltimore Orioles third baseman
Jerry Jones, Dallas Cowboys owner
Cotton Cordell, fishing lure maker
Paul Klipsch, Klipsch speaker inventor
Scott Bond, black agricultural leader
Kemmons Wilson, Holiday Inn founder
John Rust, cotton picker inventor
Conrad Harington, FM radio inventor
Tom Butt, jurist
Ed and **Pat Matthews**, missionaries
Louise Thaden, aviation pioneer
Sam Walton, Wal-Mart founder

Appendix Two

County	Created	County Seat
Arkansas	1813	De Witt & Stuttgart
Ashley	1848	Hamburg
Baxter	1873	Mountain Home
Benton	1836	Bentonville
Boone	1869	Harrison
Bradley	1840	Warren
Calhoun	1850	Hampton
Carroll	1823	Berryville & Eureka Springs
Chicot	1823	Lake Village
Clark	1818	Arkadelphia
Clay	1873	Corning & Piggott
Cleburne	1883	Heber Springs
Cleveland	1873	Rison
Columbia	1852	Magnolia
Conway	1825	Morrilton
Craighead	1859	Jonesboro & Lake City
Crawford	1820	Van Buren
Crittenden	1825	Marion
Cross	1862	Wynne

County	Created	County Seat
Dallas	1845	Fordyce
Desha	1838	Arkansas City
Drew	1846	Monticello
Faulkner	1873	Conway
Franklin	1837	Charleston & Ozark
Fulton	1842	Salem
Garland	1873	Hot Springs
Grant	1869	Sheridan
Greene	1833	Paragould
Hempstead	1818	Hope
Hot Spring	1829	Malvern
Howard	1873	Nashville
Independence	1820	Batesville
Izard	1825	Melbourne
Jackson	1829	Newport
Jefferson	1829	Pine Bluff
Johnson	1833	Clarksville
Lafayette	1827	Lewisville
Lawrence	1815	Walnut Ridge
Lee	1873	Marianna
Lincoln	1871	Star City
Little River	1867	Ashdown
Logan	1871	Booneville & Paris
Lonoke	1873	Lonoke
Madison	1836	Huntsville
Marion	1835	Yellville
Miller	1820	Texarkana
Mississippi	1833	Blytheville & Osceola
Monroe	1829	Clarendon
Montgomery	1842	Mount Ida
Nevada	1871	Prescott

County	Created	County Seat
Newton	1842	Jasper
Ouachita	1842	Camden
Perry	1840	Perryville
Phillips	1820	Helena
Pike	1833	Murfreesboro
Poinsett	1838	Harrisburg
Polk	1844	Mena
Pope	1829	Russellville
Prairie	1846	Des Arc & DeValls Bluff
Pulaski	1818	Little Rock
Randolph	1835	Pocahontas
St. Francis	1827	Forrest City
Saline	1835	Benton
Scott	1833	Waldron
Searcy	1838	Marshall
Sebastian	1851	Fort Smith & Greenwood
Sevier	1828	DeQueen
Sharp	1868	Ash Flat
Stone	1873	Mountain View
Union	1829	El Dorado
Van Buren	1833	Clinton
Washington	1828	Fayetteville
White	1835	Searcy
Woodruff	1862	Augusta
Yell	1840	Danville & Dardanelle

Appendix Three

Arkansas' Largest Cities

City	Population
Little Rock	175,795
Fort Smith	72,798
North Little Rock	61,741
Pine Bluff	57,140
Jonesboro	46,535
Fayetteville	42,099
Hot Springs	32,462
Springdale	29,941
Jacksonville	29,101
West Memphis	28,259
Conway	26,481
Rogers	24,692
El Dorado	23,146
Blytheville	22,906
Texarkana	22,631
Russellville	21,260
Sherwood	18,893
Paragould	18,540
Benton	18,177
Searcy	15,180

ARKANSAS' SMALLEST TOWNS

Town	Population
Patmos	32
Oakhaven	35
Blue Eye	38
Wiederkehr Village	42
Gilbert	43
Rudy	45
Jerome	47
Powhatan	51
Sherrill	55
Fourche	55
Reader	56
Beaver	57

Appendix Four

Some Arkansas Places and
The Origin of Their Names

Lavaca: Spanish for *cow*; given to a town near Fort Smith

L'Anguille: French for *eel*; given to a river in east Arkansas

Dorcheat: French corruption of the Caddo word for *people*; given to a stream in Columbia County

Hiwasse: Cherokee for *meadow*; given to a town in Benton County

Chickalah: a town in Yell County named for Chic-killeh, a prominent Cherokee Indian

Choctaw: a town in Van Buren County that originated near a Choctaw Indian camp

Dennard: a town in Van Buren County named for an English emigrant

Dierks: a town in Howard County named for a Danish emigrant

Bayou Meto: Quapaw for *Bear Bayou*; a stream in southeast Arkansas

Barton: a town in Phillips County named for a Swiss immigrant

Bingen: a town in Hempstead County named by a German postmaster for Bingen-on-the-Rhine in Germany

Prague: a community in Grant County named by Bohemian and Slovak immigrants for the city in the present-day Czech Republic

Subiaco: a town in Logan County named for a town in Italy

Ink: a town in Polk County named for instructions on form for establishment of post office: "fill in name in ink"

APPENDIX FIVE

ARKANSAS INFORMATION

TWELVE NATURAL WONDERS:

1. Blanchard Springs Caverns (Stone County)
2. Crater of Diamonds (Pike County)
3. Glory Hole waterfall (Newton County)
4. Mammoth Spring (Fulton County)
5. Lake Chicot (Chicot County)
6. Buffalo National River (Newton, Searcy, and Marion counties)
7. Sunken Lands (Poinsett and Craighead counties)
8. Forty-seven hot springs (Hot Springs National Park, Garland County)
9. Hawksbill Craig rock outcrop (Newton County)
10. Bear Creek Wilderness (Lee County)
11. Burns Park (North Little Rock): the second largest municipal park in the U.S., after New York's Central Park
12. Bayou Bartholomew (Jefferson, Lincoln, Desha, Drew, and Ashley counties): the longest bayou in the United States

TWELVE MAN-MADE WONDERS:

1. Tunnel of the Ozarks (Bobby Hopper Tunnel) and Interstate 540 (Crawford and Washington counties)
2. Arkansas Territorial Restoration (Little Rock)
3. Marked Tree Siphon (Poinsett County)
4. Old Washington Historic State Park (Hempstead County)
5. White River Dams—Beaver, Bull Shoals, and Norfolk (Carroll, Marion, and Baxter counties)
6. Fanciful concrete and wood sculptures at the Old Mill (North Little Rock)
7. Thorncrown Chapel (Eureka Springs, Carroll County)
8. Harahan Bridge (railroad and vehicle) (Crittenden County)
9. Arkansas River Navigation System (Fort Smith to Mississippi River)
10. Forty-story TCBY Building (Little Rock)
11. Union Pacific Locomotive No. 6938 (North Little Rock): the largest diesel-electric locomotive used on an American railroad
12. KATV television tower (Jefferson County): the second tallest structure in the world until the mid-1970s

Six Most Familiar Sites:

1. Old State House (Little Rock): where Bill Clinton twice accepted election as President of the United States
2. Razorback Stadium (Fayetteville): scene of numerous nationally televised football games
3. Little Rock Central High School
4. National Guard Professional Education Center (North Little Rock): the "West Point" of the U.S. National Guard Bureau, where thousands of National Guard personnel from every state and territory train each year
5. Villa Marre (Little Rock). Set for the CBS television series *Designing Women*
6. Jot 'Em Down Store (Pine Ridge, Montgomery County). The original was seen only in the imagination of listeners to radio's *Lum and Abner Show* for twenty-five years.

STATE FLAG

The Arkansas flag has twenty-five stars around the blue diamond border to indicate its admission to the Union as the twenty-fifth state. The four large blue stars inside the diamond signify the four governments to which Arkansas has belonged: Spain, France, the United States, and the Confederacy. The three stars below the name Arkansas also signify it was the third state formed out of the Louisiana Purchase. The flag was designed by Ms. Willie K. Hocker of Wabbaseka and officially adopted by the General Assembly in 1913.

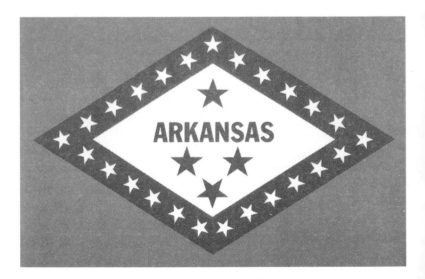

ARKANSAS FACTS

State Motto: *Regnat Populus*—The People Rule
State Mammal: White Tail Deer
State Bird: Mockingbird
State Gem: Diamond
State Flower: Apple Blossom
State Fruit: Pink Tomato
State Tree: Pine
State Insect: Honeybee
State Population: Approximately 2.4 million at end of twentieth century, of which about sixty percent live in cities and towns
Highest Elevation: Mt. Magazine (Logan County), at 2,753 feet above sea level
Lowest Elevation: Ouachita River, south of Felsenthal Dam (Union County), fifty-four feet above sea level
Surface Area: 34 million acres
Forest cover: 17.7 million acres
Agricultural land: 15.6 million acres
Surface water: 0.7 million acres
Average Temperature: January—40-45 degrees, July—80 degrees
Average annual rainfall: 45-54 inches
Average sunny days: 119 per year